SAM & TEDDY
VISIT THE DENTIST

Created by Joseph & Rami Zeid
and Romney Nelson

The Life Graduate Publishing Group

No part of this book may be scanned, reproduced or distributed in any printed or electronic form without the prior permission of the author or publisher.
Copyright - The Life Graduate Publishing Group 2021 - All Rights Reserved

Contact Sam & Teddy and say hello!

Sam & Teddy would love to hear from you! If your child would like to contact Sam & Teddy to let them know if they have helped or just to say hello they can make contact at:

samandteddyadventures@gmail.com

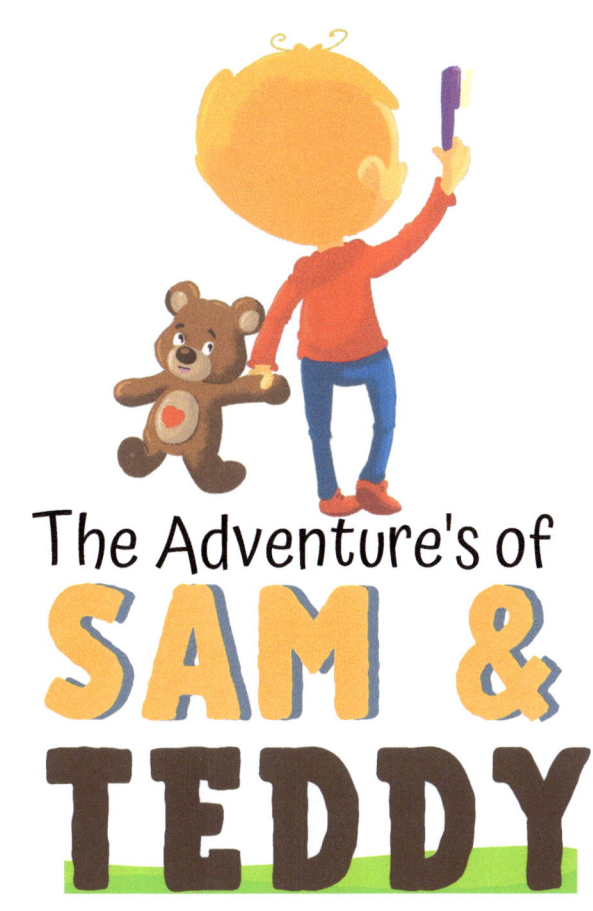

"Sam, we're off to see the dentist today,

to check your teeth are free from decay."

"Get yourself ready and brush your teeth,

just make sure to scrub up the top and underneath."

With teddy under my arm, we jump in the car.

It's only 10 minutes, so not very far.

I feel a little nervous, but I know I'm brave,

I just stand up straight and give a friendly wave.

We sit in the waiting room,
there are plenty of toys,

puzzles, books and games, they're just perfect for girls and boys.

Along comes my dentist, he's all dressed in white.

He calls out my name and I hold teddy tight!

Dentist Steve greets me with a big friendly smile.

"It's been 6 months since I've seen you, it feels like awhile."

Teddy and I walk off to the dentist room,

it has a smell of roses, just like mummy's perfume!

Jump in the chair,
and I'll give you a ride.

The slippery leather made it
feel just like a slide!

Up and down, left and right,

just be sure to hold on tight!

The dental nurse placed some glasses on my face,

she positioned them perfectly to sit in the right place.

Next to me were lot's of shiny new tools.

Only Dentist Steve can touch them. They were the rules!

There were long ones, short ones and some with flat ends.

There were even a few with some curly round bends.

"Open your mouth as wide as you can,

I'm just going to take a quick little scan".

"Now keep your mouth open, it's important to me,

I'll look at your teeth and let you know what I see".

He used his tools gently,
I hardly felt a thing.

He grabbed some dental
floss that looked like
some string.

He cleaned and polished every tooth so it was clean.

On top and behind and everywhere in between.

"Now grab that white cup and give your mouth a rinse".

It was fresh and cold and tasted like peppermints.

Dentist Steve lowered my chair and gave me the thumbs up.

He said "just spit in that white bowl and hand me your cup".

He said my teeth are looking healthy, all shiny and white,

but I must continue to brush, both morning and night.

Up I jumped from the chair, that wasn't scary at all,

in fact it was fun and enjoyable and I had a ball!

Off we go with my toothbrush and teddy.

Next time I come back in 6 months, I'll be excited and ready!

The Adventures of
SAM &
TEDDY

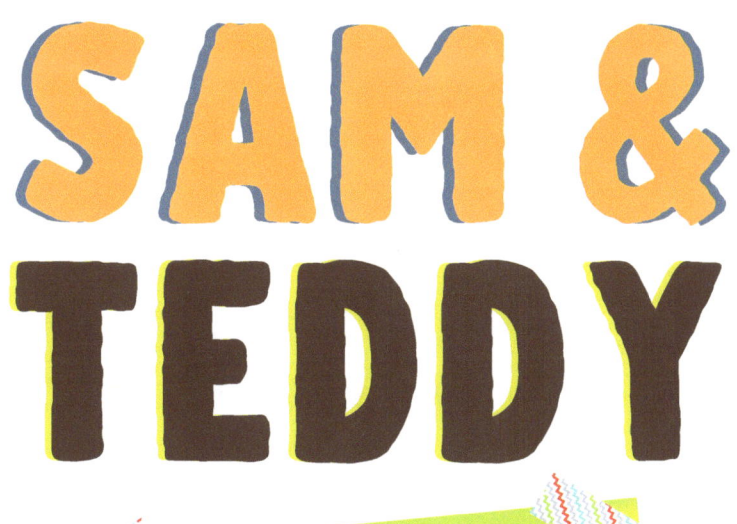

The Life Graduate Publishing Group

Email Sam and Teddy at
samandteddyadventures@gmail.com if you would like to be notified of new books in this series.

We love to receive reviews from our customers. If you had the opportunity to provide a review we would greatly appreciate it.
Thank you!

Other titles by the
The Life Graduate Publishing Group

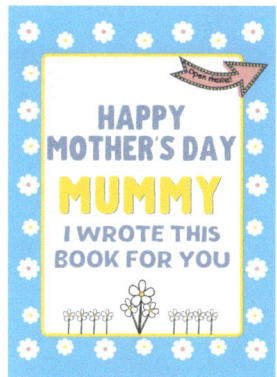

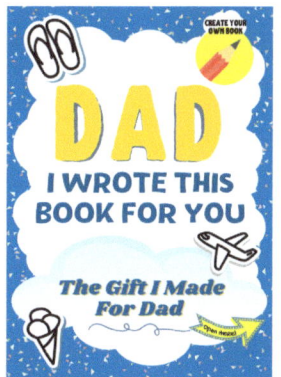

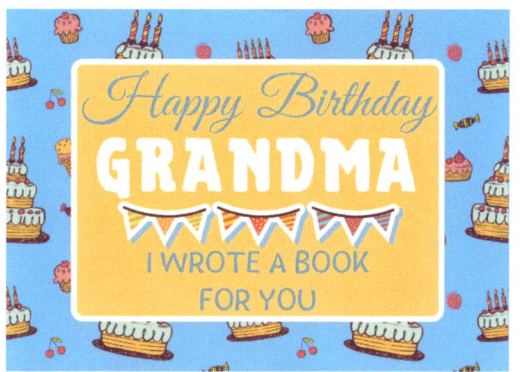

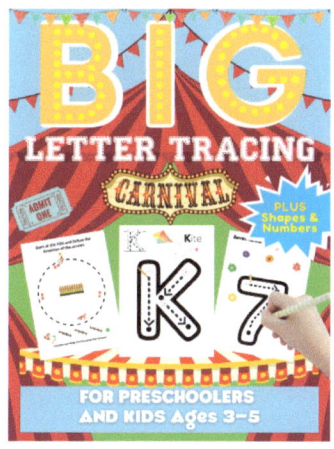
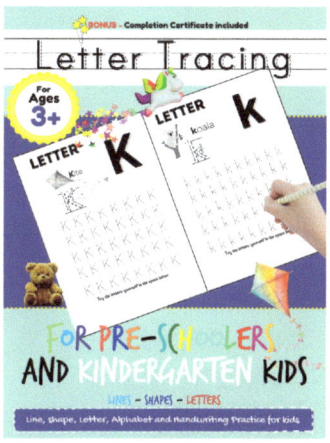
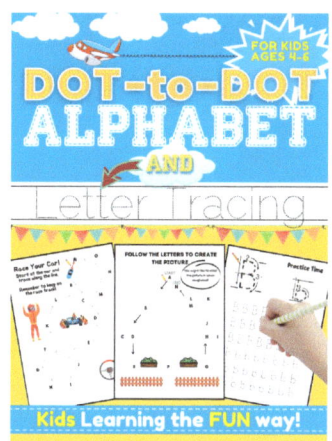

Available via major online bookstore's or via
www.thelifegraduate.com/bookstore

www.ingramcontent.com/pod-product-compliance
Lightning Source LLC
LaVergne TN
LVHW071653060526
838200LV00029B/447